FOR INTERMEDIATE PLAYERS

HOW TO BEAT YOUR FRIENDS
AT BACKGAMMON

Copyright © 2019 by Tue Rasmussen
All rights reserved. This book or any portion thereof
may not be reproduced or used in any manner whatsoever
without the express written permission of the publisher
except for the use of brief quotations in a book review.

Printed in the United States of America

ISBN: 9781676378440

First Printing, 2019

How to Beat your Friends at Backgammon Even More - From Intermediate to Advanced. 5

Introduction 5
About the author & why you should take my advice
Advanced checker play 8
- Timing 8
- Diversification 9
- Back-loaded and front-loaded 10
- Efficiency 10
- Duplication 11
- Policeman 12
- Jumping a Blockade 14
- Containment 15
- Split 17
- Slot 17
- Bear-in against an anchor - the "wave" formation .. 18
- Back game anchors 19
- Dice combinatorics 20

Pip-counting 23
- Mental-shift method 23
- Cluster counting 25

Doubling 27
- Using the cube - a quick reminder 27
- Equity 27

Doubling in matches 30
- Doubling Window & Equity with the doubling cube in play 30
- Cube ownership and market loss 32

PRAT - Position, Race, and Threats 34
Keith Count 35
The 8%, 9%, 12% rule simplified 39
O'Hagans law of market losers 40
Match equity 41
Match Equity - main take away for now 42
Match Equity advanced concepts............................. 43
Calculating match takes and passes......................... 45
Remembering the most important scores and cube efficiency... 45
Take Points at 1away scores 47

Typical doubling positions for each game strategy
Blitz 48
Blockade 49
Race 49
Waiting Game 50

Reference Positions 51
Quizzes 56
More Quizzes 63
A Special Request 63

How to Beat your Friends at Backgammon Even More - From Intermediate to Advanced.

Introduction

The second step in your backgammon journey begins now. You can no longer call yourself a complete beginner, but rather an aspiring backgammon expert! This book is meant as a follow-up to my first backgammon book "How to Beat Your Friends at Backgammon" for complete beginners that taught you the basic rules and strategies. This second book will continue in its footsteps by teaching your more advanced concepts with a high focus on getting the point across in an easy and fast way. We will cover some of the more geeky and difficult aspects of backgammon theory, but with a laser-sharp focus on the tools, you will actually use in a match. If you have not read my first book you can easily pick up this second installment and read it independently of the other.

Firstly, we will go through many advanced checker play concepts that will elevate your game to a new level.

Secondly, we will cover some pip counting methods in depth.

Thirdly, the book explains the important concepts related to the doubling cube.

Fourthly, you will be presented with some important reference positions for the cube.

The book ends with a quiz and answers section that will outline the correct way of thinking as a backgammon expert.

About the author & why you should take my advice

I started playing in 2012 after going to my first big backgammon tournament in Denmark called Nordic Open. Going there I wasn't actually very interested in backgammon but was just tagging along with a friend. Entering my name in the beginners' section I really didn't know much else then the basic rules - actually I don't even think I knew them at that time! The doubling cube was completely mysterious to me. However, I took a quick 15-minute lecture and then I was ready (maybe not). The playing area was buzzing with activity. A whole conference area was filled to the brim with backgammon boards and the shuffling sound of shaking dice cups. To this day I can still remember my first match. Believe me, I didn't have a clue what was going on in that little square board! Everything was chaotic and my brain was trying to make sense of this jumbled mess. After playing a few matches against fellow beginners I lost some and won some.

Nothing spectacular happened nor were any big prizes won that day. However, I was recruited into a local backgammon club that was looking for young members. The people there seemed nice and it turned out I was right about that and my commitment to the club grew.

In Denmark, we have a seasonal tournament where clubs play each other every week and I started out playing on a team in the 2nd division. Soon I was hooked! I started playing a lot with Extreme Gammon and practicing every aspect of the game. In my second season, I won the Danish championship in the 2nd division and my skill level was increasing steadily. After this, our club was disbanded because many players had to change priorities. This led to a few years of pause in my club career though.

I still played online and joined the team developing what is now Backgammon Galaxy. In 2017 I was again asked by an elite club in Copenhagen to join their ranks. Winning the elite division seasonal tournament might be the most difficult tournament to win in the world. I didn't expect it to happen, but that year I won the season along with my teammates!

Now I am writing this book to share the concepts and ideas that I actually use when I play backgammon to win. Many books are packed with stuff you don't need. When writing I really try to imagine myself at the beginning of my "career" where my brain was struggling to make sense of the game. I try to explain things as simply as possible. This is not quantum mechanics, but some aspects of the game are tricky to learn, so just take it easy and learn the easy stuff fast and the hard stuff slowly.

Advanced checker play

Many of these advanced checker play concepts are like smaller grained details that will improve your game when you know the basics.

Timing

This concept tells you whether or not you can hold your anchors in waiting games (also called holding- or contact games) or you should start thinking about changing strategies or breaking your anchor(s). There are situations where you will not be far enough behind in the race to hold your anchors. In such cases, you have to mobilize some spare checkers to get more timing. Doing this you give up some contact value, but it's better than breaking your anchor or your important home board points. Timing is extremely crucial in back games where you often have to be at least 70 pips behind. Timing is also important when you are caught behind a blockade. The number one largest clue for timing is simply the pip-count. Timing also comes into play if you are a good way ahead in the race. In such cases, you often have to run from your anchor or start a blitz because you do not have enough timing to hold on to your anchor.

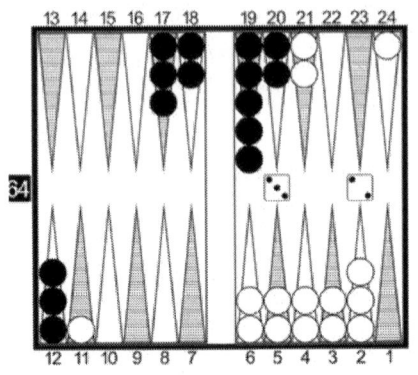

Here you see a position where we have bad timing and might have to play our policeman to the anchor before getting a shot.

- **Timing when behind in the race:** be sure you can hold onto your anchor and not crunch your home board points.
- **Timing when ahead in the race:** consider if you should try to run with a checker from your anchor (or wait for a roll more) or to possibly start a blitz.

Diversification

Diversification is the thing that makes bad players think that a good player is lucky! Diversification means that your checkers are thoughtfully (not carelessly) dispersed on many points, so you increase your chances of making new points. Diversification is strongest when you have a spare third checker on an existing point. There are also many situations where you can place a checker alone on a point just for the sake of increasing your diversification. This happens most often at the beginning of a game where the opponent's checkers are not within direct hitting range of your lone checker (more than 6 pips away).

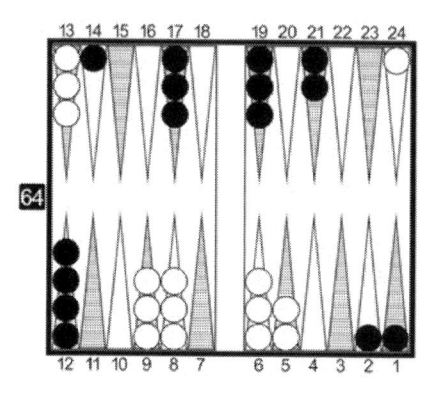

- Diversification is most important in the opening game as we fight to build new points.
- Diversification works best when you have checkers on existing points or lone checkers outside the direct reach of your opponent.

Back-loaded and front-loaded

This concept is simply a very typical consideration of the diversification principle. When you create diversification try to do it on the backmost points of your home board position rather than on the front. Frontloading does create short term diversification, but it can backfire in the longer term as front-loaded checkers typically can be part of fewer potential points.

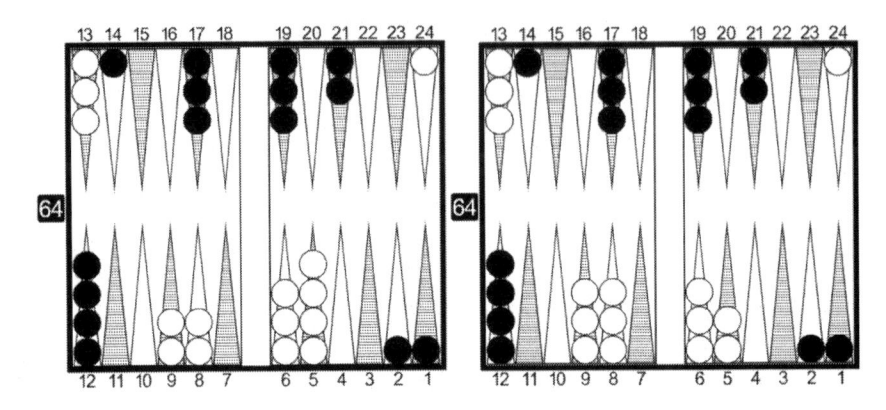

Here you see a front-loaded position and a back-loaded position.

- There are fewer good rolls than if had the checkers been on the backmost points.
- Always choose to backload rather than frontload when you can.

Efficiency

Efficiency is a general concept that is also closely associated with diversification. Efficiency tells us that we have to use every roll and every move of the dice as best as possible to win. You could see your checkers as your little toy soldiers that you need to put to use if you want to win the war! Concretely, this entails that we do not like to have huge stacks of checkers on single points. We want them diversified and ready to run, make new points, block or hit our opponent. Efficiency is most important at the beginning of a game where we naturally have two stacks of 5 checkers. We should try to do something productive with these extra checkers rather than letting them sit idle on two big stacks of points. The only scenario where we accept inefficiency is if we are far ahead in the race and purely want to avoid getting hit and sent back, or if we are very afraid of the opponents strong home board position (when we have a "weak" position and she has a "strong" position).

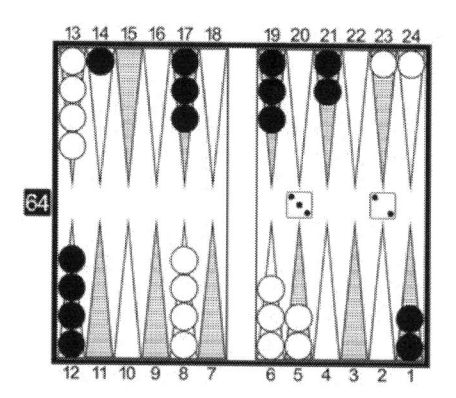

Here we have a chance to be more efficient by using the extra checker on the 8- and 13-point to create more diversification.

- Efficiency is a general term describing the use of our checkers in the pursuit of winning.
- Each checker is a resource or "toy soldier" ready to help you win.
- Efficiency specifically means using checkers to diversify, build points or hitting. Inefficiency is idle stacked checkers and semi-dead or dead checkers on the 1-point.

Duplication

This concept is very tactical as you only consider the consequences of the next roll of your opponent and not the "distant" future (opposed to a strategy where we consider long term goals). Duplication means that when you have to leave a "shot" (a potentially good roll for your opponent that can hit your checker) multiple places on the board you place your checker in such a way that you minimize the good rolls of your opponent. In practice, this often means that you make sure the opponent can only hit with e.g. 3s rather than 3s and 4s. In this way, you "duplicate" the places on the board where a 3 is good for the opponent. This is great as she can only use a roll of the dice one time. The only time duplication backfires is if your opponent rolls a double corresponding to the number you duplicated, but it always pays to duplicate if you can't simply play your checker to safety.

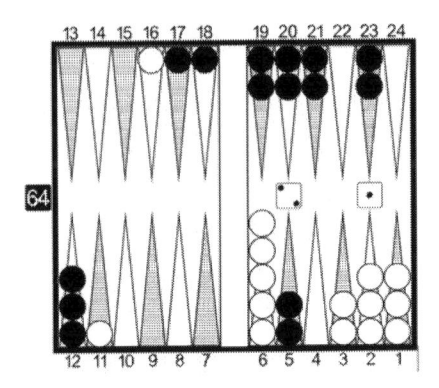

Here you see a classic example of a position where we need to consider duplication. By playing 11/9 the opponent can only use 4s directly rather than the original 6s and 4s!

- Dice combinatorics is a key skill for duplication positions (more on that soon).
- Duplication is often important when avoiding to get hit.
- Often you must also count in-direct shots.

Policeman

The policeman is a lone checker sitting all the way behind in the opponent's home board. It is part of a waiting game where we do not have an anchor. Instead, we settled for this single policeman checker. Usually, the policeman is usually left waiting unless the opponent starts having a very strong inner board as the risk of being hit and closed out (having one or more checkers on the bar and all the opponent's inner board points being closed) would be too high. We also play the policeman to safety if we get back into the race.

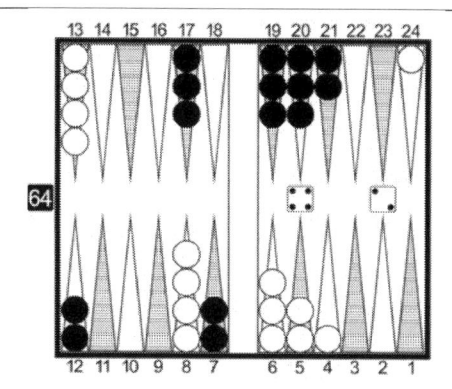

Here we do not really like having a single exposed checker. However, it also has enough value as part of a waiting game strategy as long as we are behind in the race.

- The policeman is only used when you are behind in the race.
- The policeman is a sort of risky waiting game.
- It is better to have a decent anchor rather than a single policeman.

Mobility

This concept is a subconcept of timing but related to very specific positions. Mobility is important to consider when your opponent has a blockade in front of your anchor and backmost checkers. Simply, your backmost checkers should be mobile rather than immobile when you start lacking timing in other parts of the board or if you are simply ahead in the race. This often means that you sacrifice some contact by playing checkers to the edge of a blockade in order to jump out. It can also imply playing a policeman checker to an anchor.

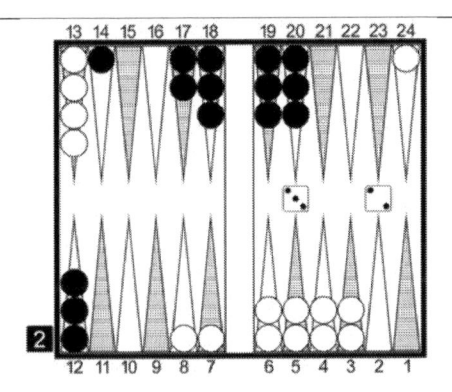

Here we need to "step up" to the 22-point with our policeman as we then get more rolls to jump out with.

- Stepping up creates more direct rolls to jump out i.e. "mobility".
- Do not step up to the edge of a blockade unless strictly necessary as it is often very valuable for the opponent to hit and expand his blockade at the edge.
- Be most aware of mobility when the race is close or if you are ahead in the race as we need to be able to run home rather than wait for a shot.

Jumping a Blockade

Most players hugely underestimate the blocking power of blockades. In the below position white actually need 6 rolls on average to jump the blockade!

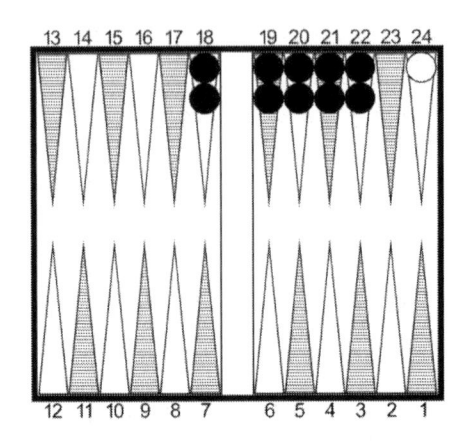

If you are behind even a four-point blockade don't assume you have plenty of time to get out. If you get the chance - step up to get direct numbers for jumping out! Remember this is most important if you are leading the race or if the race is close.

Now you know this simple yet powerful piece of knowledge that will improve your understanding of timing and mobility against blockades.

Containment

A common situation in backgammon is when you are far ahead in the race, but the opponent gets lucky and hits one of your checkers when you are bearing off. In this situation the opponent's job is now to "contain" the checker i.e. to not let it run back to safety. This is actually more difficult than it seems, and the checker is often said to be "slippery as an eel". Great containment play is a bit like diversification, but we often do not care if our checkers are placed on points or as lone checkers. Just spread out your checkers so you have more rolls to hit or catch "the eel"!

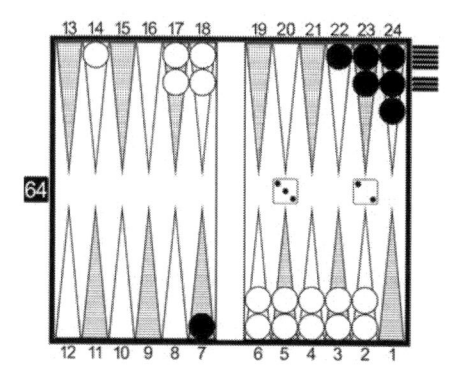

Here we should play 18/16, 18/15. Notice that we block his 55 and we do not mind getting hit as we can hit back from the bar.

- Spread out your checkers as much as possible unless the opponent still has a good inner board.
- Make points if you can block the opponent's doubles like 44, 55 or 66.

- You can be more aggressive if the opponent has a lone checker in her inner board, as this would create hits from the bar when entering, should the opponent hit us.
- The most optimal distance away from a lone checker is 12 pips. This maximizes the potential for getting a direct shot after the opponents roll. For example, in the above position, the most optimal spot would be the 19-point.

Pay now or pay later

This relates to the common scenario when we have escaped our backmost checkers to the midpoint (13-point) and the opponent is playing a waiting game. When we start lacking timing, we begin to consider whether to break our backmost point (pay now) or wait for a roll or two (pay later). Usually, we pay later, but there are a few things to consider. Is the opponent's home board (points 1-6) strong or weak, or is she about to improve her home board a lot on her next roll? If she is weak, we can more often take a risk and try to break away, by "paying now", if she is strong it's best to "pay later".

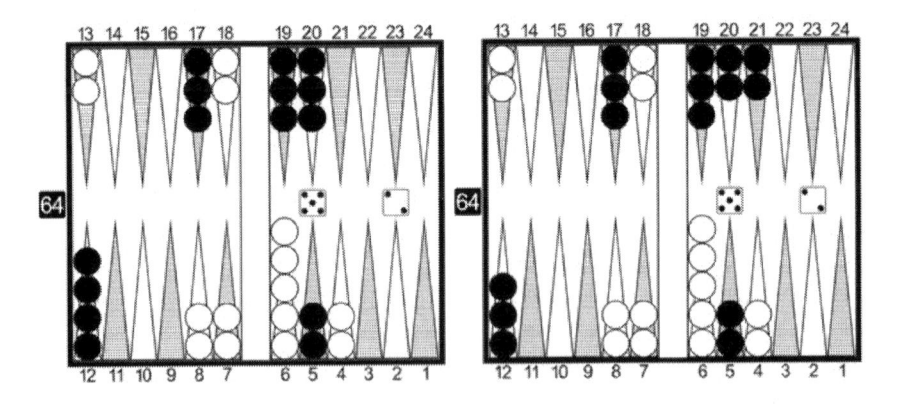

The first position is a pay now scenario and the second is a pay later scenario. There are two deciding factors. The first is that black stands to improve her board in the next roll, and secondly is the strength of his inner board. In the second position, the potential for having a strong inner board has materialized and it's too dangerous to pay now.

- It's usually correct to pay later. We are waiting to get a good double that makes running away easy.

- To pay now is most often correct when our inner board is relatively strong compared to our opponent's.

Split

Splitting mostly refers to breaking up your initial 24-point anchor in the opening part of the game. Normally, the pip count is quite equal in the first few rolls of the game and both players split to try to gain an advanced anchor. Usually, we should try to split if we are ahead or equal in the race, or if our opponent has split. If we are suddenly a lot behind in the race we should stay put! This usually only happens if the opponent rolls a high double. There are many ways to split to the 23-, 22-, 21-, -20 or 18-point. All of them are often great ways to split

- Try to split in the opening game to gain an advanced anchor. The best are the 18-, 20- and 21- point anchors. Only the 23-anchor is weak.
- Be more eager to split if your opponent has split herself.
- Do not split if your opponent gets a high double in the early roll as this shifts your strategy toward a waiting game we do not want to activate his blitz strategy.
- If you split towards a blockade, try not to split to the edge of it, unless you have no choice.

Slot

A slot is when we put a lone checker on a point in order to prepare to make it in the next roll if the lone checker is not hit. Naturally, this can be risky as it means putting a checker in direct line of the opponent. Slotting is an advanced and risky type of checker play that it is often worth it in the opening game. When we slot we have usually been hit once or twice, putting us behind in the race. Since we are behind in the race and no longer afraid of losing more pips we can try the risky slots. The common point to slot is your 5-point or 7-point. Do not slot when your opponent has a strong home board as his blitzing value is then too high.

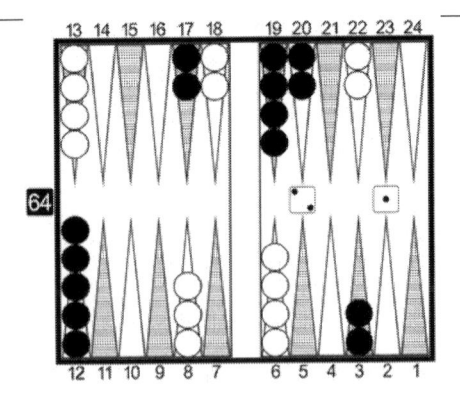

Here we play 6/5 and 13/11. Notice how we are far behind in the race (something we can quickly see by comparing the anchors. We have four men sent back while the opponent only has two) and are quite secure with our two anchors.

- Slot when you are behind in the race.
- Slot when you are not going to be "weak" on both sides of the board. This means you can slot more freely if you have an advanced anchor.
- If you have a back game, you have complete freedom to slot as you are not at risk of being closed out.

Bear-in against an anchor - the "wave" formation

If we are lucky enough to have put all of our checkers into our home board, and our opponent still has a deep anchor on our 1-point (often referred to as an ace point game), we have to place our checkers in a special way. We put them in a wave pattern that guards against rolling bad numbers that leave shots.

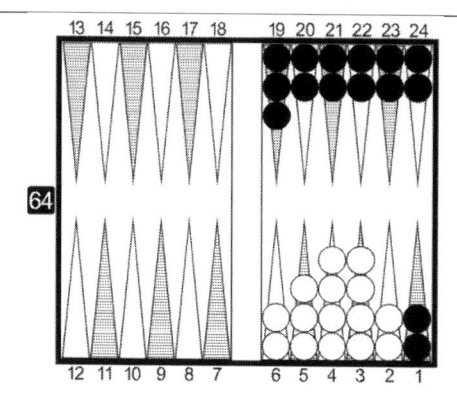

When you start clearing points you should continue using the wave pattern idea but try not to load up too many checkers on the 2-point.

Back game anchors

Back games are variations of waiting games where we have two or more anchors back in our opponent's home board hence the name "back". Not all back games are equal in strength. To play a back game we should have enough timing by being at least 70 pips behind. Furthermore, we should have a good anchor setup as not all anchors are of equal strength. In the below positions you will see a strong setup and a weaker setup. The strongest setup is when:

- The anchors are close together.
- Are placed higher in the inner board. If you are very far behind it can be just fine to have the back game on the lower inner board points.
- Both anchors have full contact with the opponent's points.

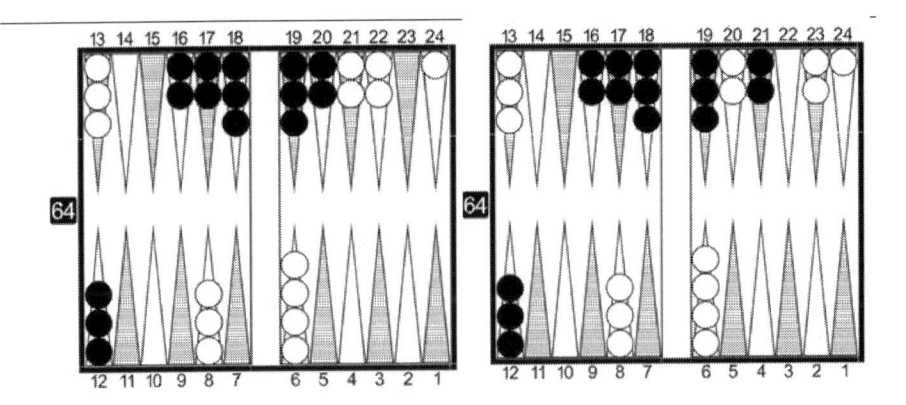

Is this an exhaustive explanation of black games? Nope! But back game territory is maybe the most complicated aspect of backgammon where even the most skilled players make huge blunders. If you know these basic aspects of the back game and your opponent doesn't you really got a tasty edge!

Dice combinatorics

Dice combinatorics simply refers to counting the number of rolls that does something we want to achieve or avoid on the board – minimizing or maximizing a probability. Usually, we count rolls that hit us or rolls that make a point. If we count rolls in certain positions we can make tactical improvements to the way we move our checkers. Look at this table to get a feel for the different rolls we can get:

As you can see there is one way to get doubles and two ways to get all other rolls. In total there are 36 different rolls. Counting rolls is not difficult with just a little practice and very crucial in certain positions. The way you can do it is by counting mentally and using your fingers to keep track. One finger is worth two rolls. First, you count non-doubles, then the doubles and add 1 for each double. Mentally you can count eg. like this while looking at the board:

"12, 13, 14, 15, 16, 23 hits (fold one finger), 24, 25, 26, 34 hits (fold another finger), 35, 36, 45, 46, 56. Okay, so four, now let me count the double...11, 22, 33, 44 hits, 55, 66. Okay, 4 plus 1 is 5 rolls that hit."

Obviously, you can also start with the highest numbers just as you please. Furthermore, it's a good reference to remember that for each number there are 11 different pairings (eg. 11, 12, 21, 13, 31, 14, 41, 15, 51, 16, 61). This is useful because we often have to evaluate the consequences of one single number from direct hits. Likewise, for two direct hitting numbers, there are 20 pairings. Remembering these two references will make counting much faster:

Number of direct shots	Number of rolls	Rolls example
1	11	12, 13, 14, 15, 16, 11 (all 1s)
2	20	12, 13, 14, 15, 16, 11 23, 24, 25, 26, 22 (all 1s and 2s)

Bonus: Convert rolls to percentages

If you want to convert rolls to percentages, I got an easy mental calculation method. Each roll is worth 2,8%, but this is difficult to multiply within your head. Instead, multiply by 3 and subtract 10%. You will be extremely close to the correct percentage value each time! An example: 8 rolls to percentage is 3x8 = 24%, 24-2.4 (10% of 24) = 21,6%. The exact value is 2.8x8 = 22,4. Not bad for something so easy!

Let's look at a typical position where we count rolls:

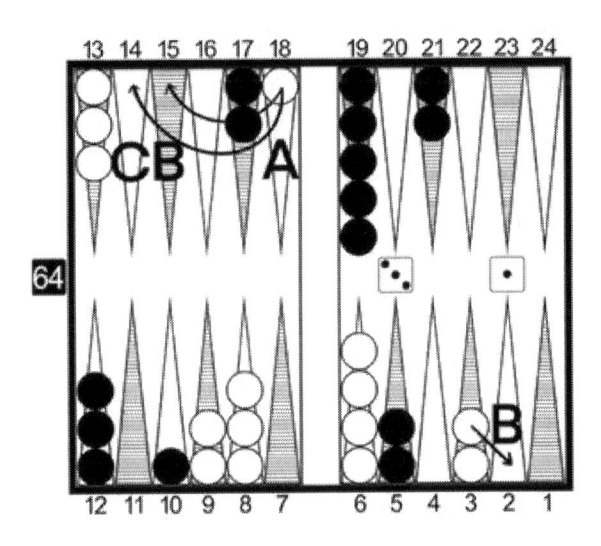

A. Starting point. Numbers that hit: all 6s and 1s (20 rolls), 42, 33, 44 = 26 rolls
B. Alternative B has 26 hits.
C. Alternative C Has 24 hits.

As you can see, first you count the numbers you know from the references of the direct shots, then you count the additional rolls, and "fly-shots" – the hits from checkers not in direct line of sight of the lone checker. In Scenario C for example, there is one roll, 63, that is a fly-shot from the 5-point.

Generally, it's often the case that moving your checker closer to the opponent's checkers will leave fewer shots, as long as you don't move it into the direct line of sight of another checker.

Pip-counting

It's time to conquer this thing with the weird name "pip" which is the measurement unit if the race. It's a little tough to get started, but everybody can learn to count pips! Just find the method you like. Personally, I am not a math person, so the following method called mental shift is perfect for me. Others do "cluster counting" as easy as breathing. If you practice any method 10 minutes a day for a week or two you will make great improvements. It's definitely easier to practice with a physical board so try that out first. Counting pips becomes much more important if you start playing with the cube, so in the end, you have to learn it. Don't worry, it can actually become a fun activity to do!

Mental-shift method

The mental shift method is like riding a bike. In the beginning, you fall, but when you learn, it's as easy as...riding a bike!

The method entails looking at the board and mentally moving your checkers to match your opponent's position, as you do this step by step you keep a running count of the difference in pip count. It is easiest if you begin by comparing your anchors to your opponent, then the midpoint and so forth. If the opposing sides are almost symmetrical you can do in seconds. Let's look at an example:

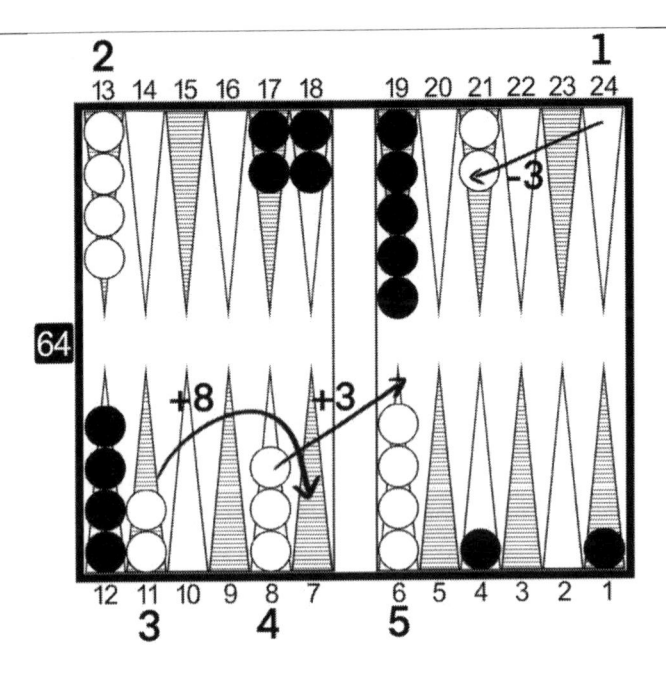

My mental process is like this:

1. Compare anchors: *seeing that one of my anchor checkers is three pips ahead of his backmost checker* thinking: "three pips ahead".
2. Compare midpoints: "same, no change".
3. Compare outfield blots. *Seeing that the closest checkers are by moving 4 pips to the 7-point*. "4 times 2 checkers = 8, three minus eight. Five behind.
4. *Seeing one checker too much on the 8-point. Shift to the 6-point where one checker is missing*. "Two pips behind. five minus two. Seven pips behind".
5. No change to the inner board. Seven pips behind in total.

It's good to remember a few references:
- There are 11 pips from the 24-point to the 13-point.
- Checkers shifted from one color point to the same color is always counted with equal numbers, and likewise, checkers shifted to a different color are counted with odd numbers. This little fact makes it easier on the brain to count.

When not to do the mental shift method? When your position and your opponent's position is not similar, it no longer makes sense to do a mental shift count, as it will be too complicated to count. In race positions, it is most often best to count the absolute pip count and not just the difference.

Cluster counting

Cluster counting entails remembering some typical checker formations and their corresponding pip-counts. If you learn enough typical formations, you can easily add clusters of pips together in your head. The advantage of this method is that you get the absolute pip counts and not just the difference, the drawback is that you must count both sides of checkers to calculate the difference. I usually only count the absolute pips when both I and my opponent have all our checkers on our home boards. Let's look at some typical clusters:

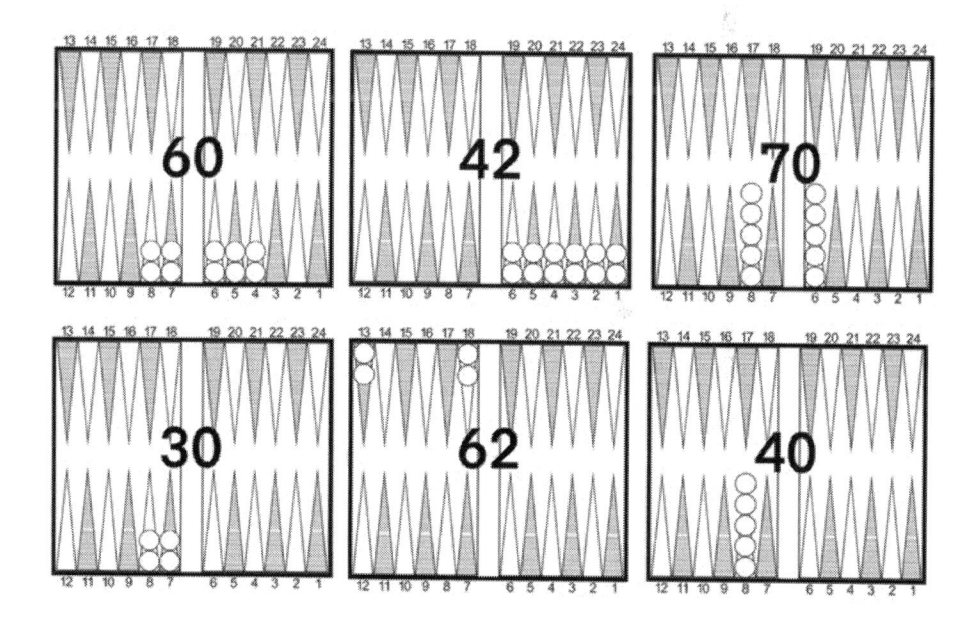

Bonus: Running pip-count in races

During a straight race, it is very useful to do a running pip-count as you often have to make a doubling consideration at each new roll. Simply you start out by doing one of the prior counts and for the following rolls, you just add or subtract the count of the dice.

Bonus Bonus: Intuitive pip count

Many times, you just have to intuitively compare your position to the opponent's position to get a clear picture of who is leading the race. The clearest indicator is who has the most checkers in the opponent's home board.

Doubling

The doubling cube is something that takes backgammon to a whole new level, both in fun and skill. Conquering the cube is the hardest thing even for world-class players. Even the best players make huge doubling mistakes from time to time which is part of the magic of backgammon. I will offer you some very handy frameworks for making better doubling decisions. If you practice these frameworks you will go from a crawl to a run in a short time. If you want to improve your skills from there you have to do what the best players do - practice with the computer for years and years! When reading the following section notice that in backgammon lingo we often say "to cube" interchangeably with "to double".

Using the cube - a quick reminder

At the beginning of a game, the cube is always placed in the middle of the board to the side or on the divider bar on the board. If a player has an advantage in the game, he or she can double the stakes before rolling the dice, by placing the cube in the middle of the playing surface with the number 2 facing upwards. Now the opposing player has to decide if she should take or pass the cube. If she passes, she loses 1 point or if she takes, the game continues onwards but with the stake of 2 instead of 1. Furthermore, since she took the cube, she now has sole ownership of it until she decides to double herself if the opportunity arises. When a new game begins the cube is always reset to the middle of the board so that both players can make the initial double to 2.

Equity

When we play backgammon there is no option of playing for nothing. The least you can play for is going from 0 to 1 fictional point and possibly winning bragging rights. We could also theoretically play for 1 dollar, 1 fish or whatever crazy thing you might imagine. The way to think about *the value* of the thing we are playing for is using the term *equity*. If you have a backgammon program you will undoubtedly have seen this number and wondered what it meant. Equity in backgammon in its most simple form as a 1 point match is expressed by a value between 0 and 1. Depending on the thing that is at stake this represents the expected value of the position you are in during a game. The value is expressed by this simple probability function that is used in many areas outside backgammon too:

Expected value = Value from good scenarios - loss of value from bad scenarios

or in a 1-point match:

Expected value = Probability of winning x Value of match - Probability of losing x Value of match

In longer matches, you also must account for gammons and backgammons which makes the function a little more complicated.

Let's say your equity in a position is 0.7 when we have accounted for the probabilities of winning, losing, gammons and backgammons, etc.

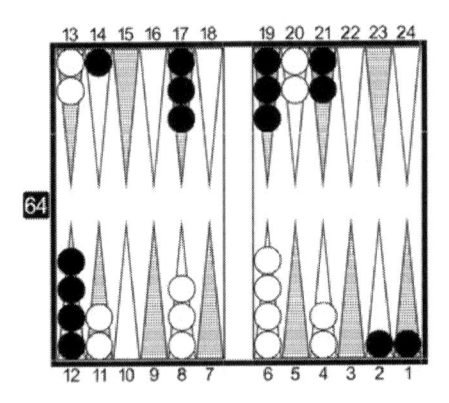

Here you see a 1-point match example where white leads. The equity for white is 30.9 % or 0.309 of a point. It's a simple example because we do not have to account for gammons or backgammons. We get 30.9% by subtracting blacks winning probability from white:

65.4 – 34.5 = 30.9

The number 0.7 could mean that your position is worth 70% of the fish you have at stake, or 70 cents of a dollar. When the game is over the winner's equity is 1 or 100% of the dollar or fish at stake and 0 for the loser.

Hopefully, this seems pretty straight forward, and we will build upon this knowledge to understand how the doubling cube doubles the equities played for.

Doubling in matches

Doubling Window & Equity with the doubling cube in play

When and how we double is connected to the term of equity and the underlying probabilities of a backgammon position. Now imagine that we turn on the concepts of gammon, backgammon and use the doubling cube. The initial stake of the game is a fish, and the initial equity can go from 0 to 1 fish. But if one player uses the doubling cube (by placing it on the board before rolling his dice) and the other player accepts the cube the stakes are now 2 fish instead of 1! Furthermore, it's now possible to win or lose up to 6 fish due to backgammons that triple the score. In theory, we could keep doubling the stakes at each turn, but in practice, the cube rarely reaches a value higher than 4 but occasionally it reaches 8 or 16. In practice, the players would probably also be playing for something tangible rather than an infinite sum of fish or dollars.

So when should you double and when should you take or pass?

The take or pass decision:

The reward from taking should be worth the risk! This boils down to a simple equation:

Take point = risk / (risk + reward)

In normal play (not a match) where the cube can only be used once (usually we can use it more than once, of course, we are just building up from a simple example), you can double up until you have a 75% winning chance and you can take if you have a 25% or more winning chance. Why 25%?

Imagine that out of 100 double offers to 2, you take every one of them, and you win 25% of those takes. Your net points would be 75 games lost - 25 games won (150 points - 50 points) or 50 games lost (100 points lost). If you had passed every double offer to 2 you would have also lost 100 points!

Let's imagine that we take a cube to 2, by mistake, when we only have 20% chances of winning: 80 games lost - 20 games won (160 points lost - 40 points won) or 60 games lost net (120 points). If we had correctly passed 100% of all the doubles, we would have lost only 100 points!

The take point calculation for this is simply:

$$25\% = 25\% / (25\% + 75\%)$$

Or in more literal terms

$$25\% = \text{Going from 25\% to 0\%} / (\text{Going from 25\% to 0\%} / \text{going from 25\% to 100\%})$$

This is the most barebone example of the take or pass decision. As we will soon get into there are other factors that impact the take point.

The doubling decision:

The doubling decision can be boiled down to an equation that is similar to the take point equation where we calculate the minimum doubling point:

Minimum doubling point:

$$\text{Min. Doubling Point} = \text{Loss from doubling} / (\text{Loss from doubling} + \text{Gain from doubling})$$

Or

$$\text{Min. Doubling Point} = \text{doubling and losing} / (\text{doubling and losing} + \text{doubling and winning})$$

No matter the winning chances you input this calculation comes to 50% meaning that we should double when we have at least a 50% win probability. But in reality, we don't do this which leads to the question:

Why not just double when we are at the minimum doubling point? Let's dive into that:

Cube ownership and market loss

The first factor that makes us not want to necessarily double at the minimum doubling point is the value of cube ownership. The cube is a weapon that has an inherent value because you can make your opponent pass or "drop" the cube whereby you win a point. If you double you give the sole ownership of this weapon to your opponent, which she can now use against you in the future. So, as you double you exercise the cube as a weapon, but at the same time you are giving some value away because you can no longer use it yourself. This means that, opposed to our prior example, we can take lower than 25% because the cube gives us some inherent equity as a weapon later on.

We talk of a cube being "live" or "dead". A cube is dead in situations where the player holding it can no longer double in any scenario. This could happen for example if you are doubled to 2 when you are leading 3-0 in a 5-point match or if you are doubled before your opponent's last roll in a game. A live cube is simply a cube that is still in play to be used, by one or both players.

The second factor is the most important. If your opponent still has a take at your next turn when you double, you can just wait to that turn to reconsider whether you should double or not. If there is a probability that your position can become too good for your opponent to accept you are in danger of losing your market. That is in other words, the window in which your opponent is willing to accept a double from you. The below figure outlines this concept graphically:

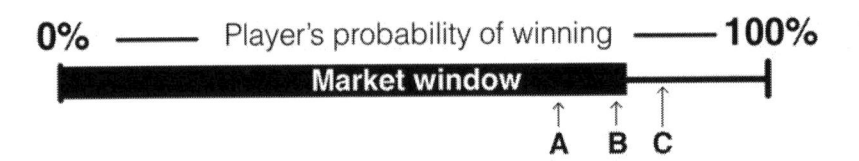

0% ──── Player's probability of winning ──── 100%

Market window

↑ ↑ ↑
A B C

A. A is our initial win probability before rolling the dice.

B. Scenario B shows a situation where we rolled a great number though it did not improve our win probability beyond the market window.

C. Scenario C is a different position where our roll gave us a huge leap in win probability beyond the point where our opponent was willing to accept a cube. Generally, when we are at a point A, we should have 9 or more rolls (O'Hagan's Law) that would take us to point C before we can double. For example, If we were at point A and only had 2 market losing rolls like 55 and 66 we cannot yet double. Remember that "good" here is defined by "rolls now that will make it unable for our opponent to take a double at our next turn". How do you know if your opponent can take? Well, you can't know for sure – it's something you have to analyze and make your opinion about. As mentioned earlier, you can look for rolls that would be "devastating" or very bad for your opponent. Often this entails:

- Rolls that hit AND make a point in your inner board.
- Rolls that would give you a race lead too big for your opponent to take.
- Rolls that make or expand a great blockade structure.

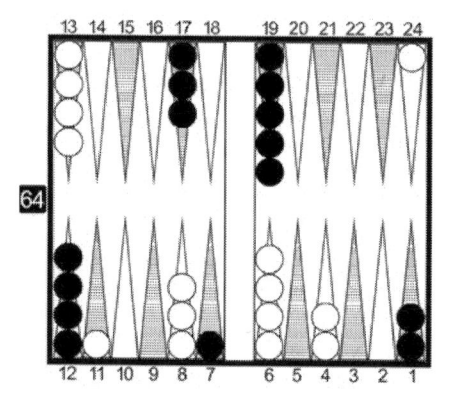

Here White has 14 market losers:

64, 41, 61, 63, 11, 33, 66, 44, 55.

The double decision is easy, and Black has a take. Not a huge take, but still the correct cube actions is still Double/Take!

We have now covered some of the basic doubling concepts and we will continue with some very useful frameworks for making decisions over the board.

PRAT - Position, Race, and Threats

This is a doubling framework that is used to analyze whether or not to double. It's really a great way to start for beginner and intermediate players rather than just going by your gut feeling! Usually, it's best used in the early to the middle part of the game and not when players are in a straight race. The rule says that you need to have an advantage in at least two of the three factors to double. If you are offered the cube you can take if the opponent does not have a lead in all three factors. If the opponent has three factors fulfilled, you have to pass. However, I would not use this rule to decide about taking or passing as it is often inaccurate. Let's try to break down the three factors for doubling.

- Position: If your position in general terms looks stronger and more robust. This accounts for home board points, high anchors, diversification of checkers, etc.
- Race: Simply, are you ahead or behind in the race? If you are just 4-5 pips ahead this factor is not yet fully fulfilled, but when you start being 10-15 or even 20 pips ahead this is sufficient.
- Threats: Do you have some strong threats if you roll that could really turn the game in your favor? This would typically be if you have some devastating blitzing opportunities, getting freedom with your back most checkers while being ahead in the race or making a strong blockade.

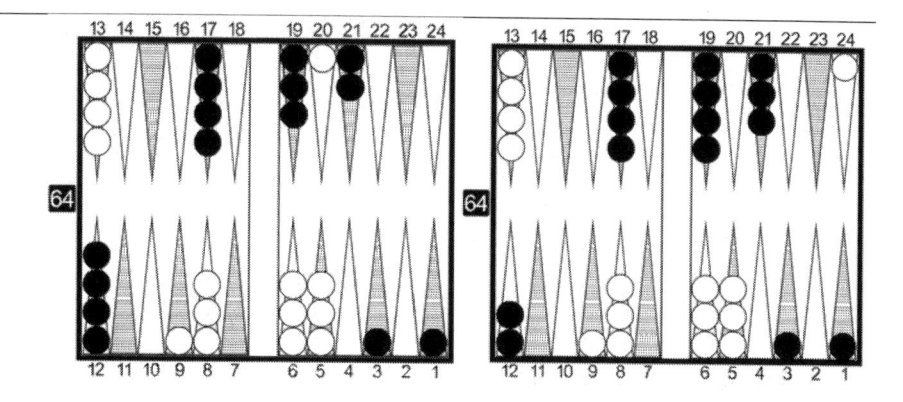

The original PRAT rule is not strong enough to use unless we make one crucial improvement!

- We should weigh the race factor stronger than the other factors. Instead of equal weights race should count for 2! In this way, PRAT is much more accurate. We need to have a substantial race lead to count this as fulfilled - a lead of 1-3 pips is not enough. Furthermore, we should have a total count of at least 3 PRAT points to double.

In the first position above we have a better position, a better race, threats to escape and to blitz. In total, we have 4 PRAT points and it's a clear double according to both PRAT and computer analysis.

In the second position, White has a better position, an equal race, and threats of blitzing and making a blockade. In total White has 2 PRAT points - not enough to double!

Keith Count

I cannot emphasize enough how strong this method is for race cubes. If you learn to do a Keith count you can go from beginner to world-class level in race cubes in one step! Remember that you should only use this method in a straight race when there is no contact left between the two players. Furthermore, I would advise you to use it only when all checkers are in their respective home boards as this is where it is strongest and the mental arithmetics is easiest. It's one of those things that looks difficult when you first try, but with a little practice, it will soon seem easy. When you know the steps by heart it's mostly a matter of adding together small numbers in your head. Before we begin, I want to mention that it's perfectly fine to skip this method and come back to it when you have mastered the simpler 10% rule written later. All these steps might seem too complicated for an intermediate or beginner. Here is how you do the Keith count:

1. First count pips for the player on roll.
2. Add 2 pips for each checker more than 1 on the 1-point.
3. Add 1 pip for each checker more than 1 on the 2-point.
4. Add 1 pip for each checker more than 3 on the 3-point.
5. Add 1 pip for each empty space on the 6-, 5- and 4-point.
6. Increase the sum by one-seventh, but round to reach a whole number.
7. Do the steps 1-6 for the opponent - leaving out adding one-seventh to the sum.
8. When you have both adjusted pip counts you calculate the difference (pip count of the player on roll – opponent's pip count).
9. Use the Keith Count rules for determining the correct decision based on the pip count difference (The rules are written further down).

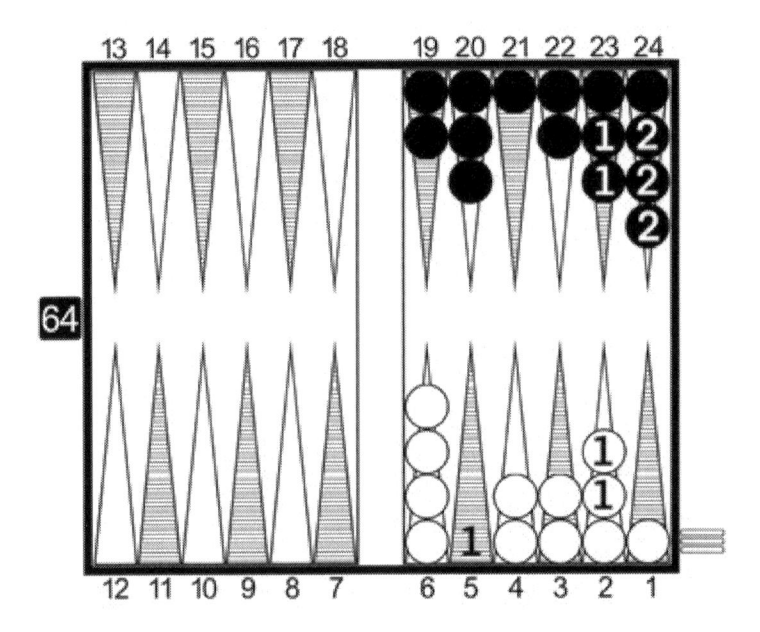

An example where the normal pip count is 45 for white and 47 for black.

1. White adds 3 to his pip count = 48. As white is on roll, we have to add one 1/7th rounded down (48/7 = 6.8 = 6). 6 is then added to 48 and white's adjusted pip count is 54.
2. For black, we just add the extra pips as she is not on roll and we, therefore, do not need to add 1/7th. Blacks adjusted pip counts comes to 55.

The final calculation is then to find the difference: 54 – 55 = -1.

Note that it is a good idea to practice the multiplication table for 7 so the 6th step is easier. Here is a table to quickly refresh the mind when needed:

Steps	Pips to add	Example: your pips - pips to add
7	1	8 - 1
14	2	19 - 2
21	3	27 - 3
28	4	28 - 4
35	5	40 - 5
42	6	47 - 6
49	7	50 - 7
56	8	56 - 8
63	9	64 - 9
70	10	71 - 10

As you can see it is important to round down rather than up! Mentally you think "My pip count is 64, okay the closest multiplication number down is 63, which means I add 9. Okay, my pip count is 63". I often use the number 70 as a reference because obviously, it's easy to remember that 7 goes into 70 ten times. You can also count from the bottom while using your fingers to keep track by folding one finger for each pip to add until you reach the closest number (rounded down) to your pip count.

9. Now you have to compare the two adjusted pip counts with the following rules:

Double:

If your pip count - opponents pip count is no higher than +4

Redouble (turning the cube from 2 to 4):

If your pip count - opponents pip count is not higher than +3

Take:

Take if the opponent's pip count exceeds your own by 2 or more.

Pass:

Pass if the doublers pip count exceeds your own by 1 or less

Phew, that's a lot of information in one bite! I often come back to just refresh my mind about the rules if I have an important match to play. Let's see a complete example:

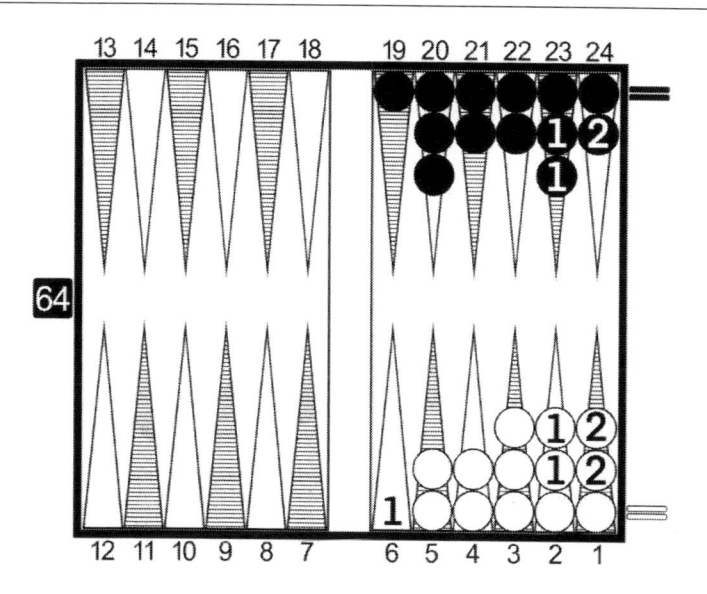

Keith Count example:

White on roll: 36 + 1 + 2 + 4 = 43. 43/7 = 6. 43 + 6 = 49.

Black: 43 + 2 + 2 = 47.

49 − 47 = +2

This is a double and a take according to the Keith Count. Which is verified by the computer analysis!

The 8%, 9%, 12% rule simplified

When the race is still so long that not all of the checkers are in the home boards I use a very simple rule that I make even simpler. The original rule is that if you are 8% percent ahead of your opponent you can double, 9% you can redouble and 12% or less behind you can take a double.

In most cases, it's sufficient to just boil it down to a 10% rule, which is very easy to manage mentally. As such, the rule is: double if you are 10% ahead, take if you are no more than 10% behind. Remember, that you should only use this rule when the race is still so far that you or your opponent still do not have all your checkers in the home board!

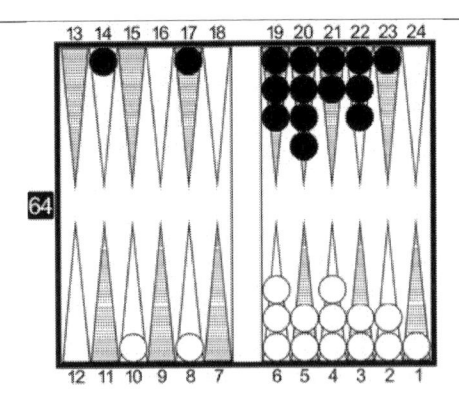

Here the pip count is 69 versus 76 meaning that we are 7 pips ahead. This is very close to 10% ahead. Calculating it is very easy as we just take 10% of 69 = 6.9 to find how much 10% is. Here it's a double and an easy take.

O'Hagans law of market losers

This is another simple rule that you can use in combination with the PRAT rule. John O'Hagan who is a great player from the US made this effective rule, that I and many others use extensively. The rule goes that you should double if you have 9 or more "market losers" after also accounting for anti-market losers. As you may remember a market loser is a roll/threat that would crush your opponent so bad that she would not be able to take a cube if you offered it in the next roll. An anti-market loser is simply a roll that is very good for your opponent. The magic sauce is knowing if the opponent should take or not, but often it will be easy to spot if the rolls are crushing or not.

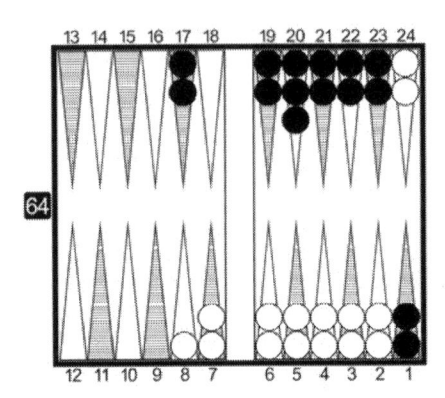

Here you see a position where white has 9 market losers. All rolls with a 6 is a market loser for a total of 11 rolls. However, 55 and 44 are devastating for white and must be subtracted for a net of 9 market losers. By definition, this is a Double/Take which is verified by computer analysis.

Match equity

Earlier we covered the basic doubling concepts. In the examples, we did not cover how to double in matches but assumed that we would be playing an infinite number of games. But how do we double in matches where we play to a set number of points?

Imagine that we are playing an actual backgammon match to 5 points. Each game of the match could be segmented into a value of 1 in equity. However, matches are always played using the doubling cube, gammons and backgammons. So we can't look at each point in an isolated fashion, but rather we have to consider our overall equity in winning the entire match ie. match equity. This is often expressed in percentages, so both players have e.g. 50% match equity at the beginning of a match at the score of 0-0 as both players have an equal probability of winning the match at this point. As the score changes the match equities change, which is extremely important to consider when doubling! The further you are ahead in the match the less aggressively you need to double and the less you will take the doubles your opponent offers you. On the other hand, you have to be more aggressive with the cube if you are far behind. This is a dynamic you may see in some sports where the trailer takes wild gambles trying to get back in the game.

The match equities at different scores can be summed up in the following match equity table:

White Needs

Black Needs	1	2	3	4	5	6	7	8	9
1	50	70	75	83	85	90	91	94	95
2	30	50	60	68	75	81	85	88	91
3	25	40	50	59	66	71	76	80	84
4	17	32	41	50	58	64	70	75	79
5	15	25	34	42	50	57	63	68	73
6	10	19	29	36	43	50	56	62	67
7	9	15	24	30	37	44	50	56	61
8	6	12	20	25	32	38	44	50	55
9	5	9	16	21	27	33	39	45	50

The table is a theoretically correct calculation of winning chances at different scores if it is assumed that both players are of equal strength and the Crawford rule is used when playing. The bold numbers in the table refer to the points the player needs to win the match, seen from the perspective of the black player. E.g. 3away/3away is 50% for each player since they need the same amount of points to win, 2away / 4away is 68% for black and 100-68 = 32% for white. Since matches can be played to a lot of different lengths (normally in odd increments like 3, 5, 7, 9, etc.) the percentages relate to the length of the match. If you have a 34% percent chance of winning your absolute equity in eg. a 5 point match is 5*34% = 1.7 points - as you may see it's easier to look at match equity as percentages.

Match Equity - main take away for now

Now you might be thinking, "Okay, so when do we actually double in matches?" We will explore this in further detail, but your main take away, for now, should simply be that you double more aggressively when behind and pass more often when you are ahead in the match. Being more aggressive with the cube already starts when you are one point behind and if you are 4-5 or more points behind you will often have to double at the slightest hint of threats! Getting a very detailed feel for this is actually impossible to teach. There is only one way to learn it in detail and that is by using the computer programs where you analyze your matches. But don't worry about that unless you are striving to become the next world champion. If you know the basics you will be far (far!) ahead of your unskilled opponent!

When behind in the match	When ahead in the match
Double more aggressively	Double more passively
Take doubles more aggressively	Take doubles more passively

Bonus - Crawford rule and Automatic doubles

The Crawford rule is always used in modern backgammon. It states that when one player reaches 1 point away from winning, the following game is played without the doubling cube. This rule gives a slight advantage to the leader of the match. If the leader does not win the Crawford game, and thereby the match, the doubling cube is introduced into the match again. At this point, post-Crawford, the trailer should double automatically in each new game. The reason for this is that the only outcome of the next games for the trailer is either losing the match or winning the game which means the risk of doubling is now zero. Post-Crawford the leader evaluates the automatic doubles as so:

Opponent points away from winning	Leader's options
2	Take if more than 50% winnings chances. Pass if less than 50%.
3	Automatic take
4	Take if more than 50% winnings chances. Pass if less than 50%.
5	Automatic take
etc.	Notice the even or uneven score is the deciding factor

Match Equity advanced concepts

All great players have an intuitive feeling of when to double after having practiced a lot with computer programs. But in the end, there are occasions when it is necessary to understand and calculate exactly when to double and when to take doubles offered by your opponent. Remembering the earlier match equity table to calculate take points is impossible for most people. For this reason, we should learn the mental tool called "Neils Numbers" named after Neil Kazaross who invented it. With this we can do some mental arithmetic to calculate match equities and derive correct cube actions (another word for the doubling, taking and pass decisions).

Calculating exact match doubles and takes with Neils numbers

3	4	5	6	7	8	9	10	11	12	13	14	15
10	9	8	7		6			5				4

The numbers in the top row represent the number of points the trailer needs to win the match. For example in a 5 point match where the trailer has 0 points he needs...5 points to win! After finding the number of points the trailer needs to win you look at the number below - in this case, it's 8. This number is multiplied by the points you are leading your opponent. Let's say that we are leading by 1 point in the 5 point match at the score of 1-0. Therefore, we multiply 1 x 8. The last step is to add this number to the percentage point of 50% and we arrive at 58%. There you have it - you have arrived at a very precise calculation of your match equity. If you look in the match equity table at black needs 4 / white needs 5 (4away/5away) you see that the calculation was correct. For reference here are the steps:

1. Note the number of points the trailer needs to win the match.
2. Note the number below.
3. Multiply the number with the number of points you are ahead of your opponent.
4. Add this number to 50% to arrive at your match equity. If you are behind you subtract from 50%.

Note that where you see an empty box you should simply take the average of the two closest numbers. For example, when a trailer needs 10 points you used 5.5 to multiply with (the average of the numbers 6 and 5).

Calculating match takes and passes

Using the Neils Numbers method we can now calculate our exact take point with the equation you learned earlier (take point = risk / (risk + reward)). Let's go through the process assuming we are playing a 5 point match and the score is 1-0 and we are doubled.

1. Reference point: Calculate the reference point if we pass. If we pass the score is 1-1 or 50% match equity.
2. Risk: Calculate the risk if we take and lose. Here the score would go to 1-2 as we lost the doubled game. At that score, we would need 4 points to win and we would be one point behind. This comes to 50 - 1 x 9 = 41% (remember we subtract if we are behind). The risk is then calculated based on the reference point if we pass: 50% - 41% = 9% (reference point from step 1 - match equity if we lose = risk).
3. Reward: Calculate the reward if we take and win. The score would then be 3-0. The Neil's number calculation would give us 3 x 8 + 50% = 74%. The reward is then 74% - 50% = 24%.
4. Take point = 9% / (9% + 24%) = 9 / 33 = 27 % (take point = risk / (risk + reward).

Therefore we would need at least a 27% winning chance to take. We would then have to evaluate our situation in the game as to whether or not we had a 27% chance of winning. As you can see at that score we have to take a little less aggressively than in normal non-match play where the take point goes down to 25%.

Remembering the most important scores and cube efficiency

To be honest, I know that all of these match equity calculations can be very confusing for a new player (and everybody else too!). But it really is an essential skill you need to learn down the line if you want to become great. But there is a super alternative! Instead of learning the whole match equity table or calculating tons of numbers in your head, we can start by learning the most important scores by heart. The important scores are those within the scope of a 5-point match such as 1away/2away, 1away/3away, etc. This is also important because gammons here can have a huge impact on the doubling decision due to what is called cube efficiency. Cube efficiency means that we should not win MORE points than we need to win the match. Let's say we need one point to win a match, but the cube is on 2 and we win that game. In this case, we risked losing 2 points and at the same time, we only needed to win one point. At the same time, it also means that in some cases we double MORE aggressively because we can reach a certain score perfectly with a cubed gammon win.

Score Normalized(absolute)	Match equity	Intuitive feel	Score nickname
4away-2away (1-3)	32%	Double extremely aggressively at the slightest threat	The Maniac
4away-3away (1-2)	41%	Double very gammonish (threatening) positions aggressively	The Tasmanian Devil
4away-5away (1-0)	58%	Double gammonish positions very aggressively	The Tasmanian Devil
3away-5away (2-0)	66%	Double less, take less	The Chicken
3away-4away (2-1)	59%	Double less, pass very easily	The Chicken
2away-5away (3-0)	75%	Almost never double unless pure race, pass easily	Scaredy Pants
2away-4away (3-1)	68%	Double only in large race leads, pass threatening positions extremely easily	Scaredy Pants Extreme
5away-4away (0-1)	42%	Pass threatening positions easily (even though we are behind we have to pass easily at this score)	The Intermezzo

5away-3away (0-2)	34%	Double gammonish positions aggressively, take deeper	**The Chihuahua**
5away-2away (0-3)	25%	Double gammonish positions very aggressively, take deeper	**The Chihuahua**

As you get more experience, these scores will almost have their own little place and personality in your memory - I gave you a jump start by giving some of them a nickname! Also, note that one of the key factors for passing or taking when ahead in the match is whether your opponent has a "gammonish" position. This is a position where the threats could easily lead to a gammon loss.

Take Points at 1away scores

In match play, we will encounter 1away - Xaway scores so often that we should remember the match equity for them by heart. The sequence goes like this for the trailing player:

1away-1away	1away-2away	1away-3away	1away-4away	1away-5away	1away-6away
50 %	32%	25%	19%	16%	12%

You don't need to remember the scores just the number sequence and then count from the top when you need it.

Typical doubling positions for each game strategy

When I look back at my early backgammon career, I remember how chaotic positions looked. It was difficult to make sense of all the patterns. For this reason, I have included an example of a typical Double/Take position for each game strategy. This is by no means exhaustive, but merely a starting point for your pattern recognition skills.

Blitz

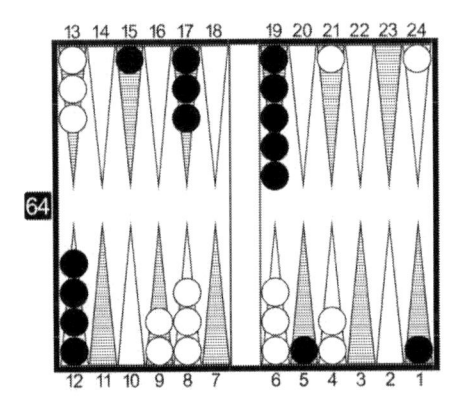

This is a double/take
- Small race lead of 8 pips
- 10 checkers in the zone
- More inner board points (stronger position than Black)
- Direct threats to hit Black
- Also, look for advanced anchors - here we don't have one, but we can still double

Blockade

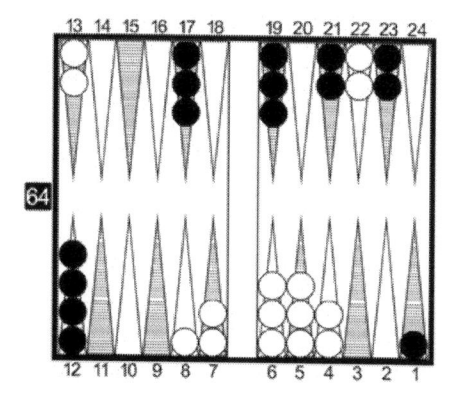

White is 5 pips behind, which is great as our main strategy here is to block! We have a solid anchor making it impossible to counter block by Black, threats to expand our prime, and a Black checker trapped. Solid double/take. Black still has a lot of time to try and escape.

Race

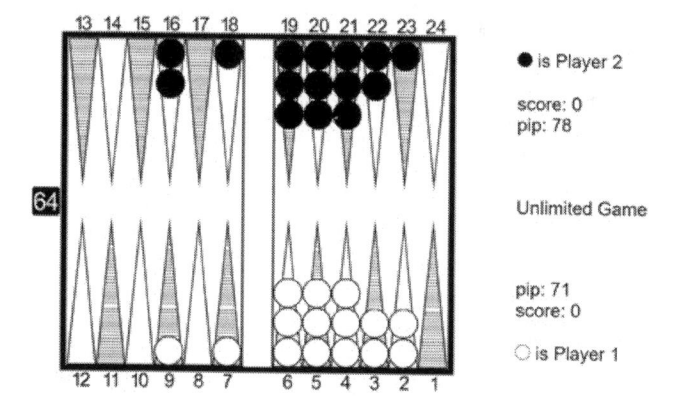

There's not a lot of stuff going on here. We simply have about a 10% race lead, which makes it natural to double and easy to take. We don't need the complicated Keith count yet.

Waiting Game

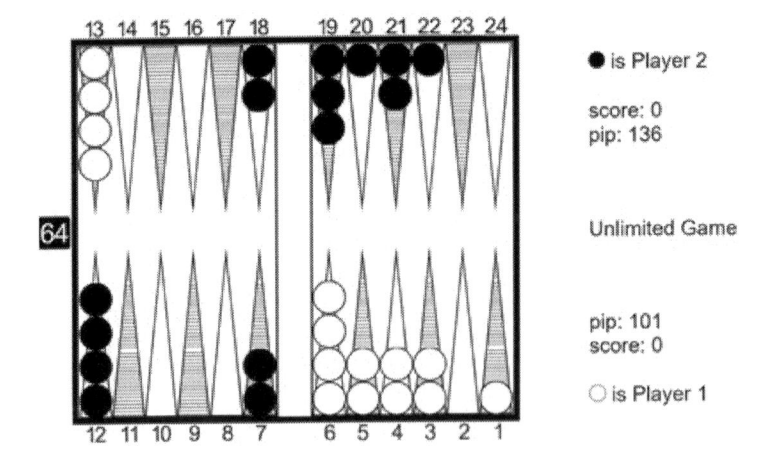

● is Player 2

score: 0
pip: 136

Unlimited Game

pip: 101
score: 0

○ is Player 1

This is such a common type of doubling decision! Here we must double as we have timing and our doubles will make it much easier to take down the midpoint. It's very important to have no more than 4 checkers on the midpoint as we can't clear away 5 checkers with our doubles. Black has an easy take as he will soon have a great inner board and time to wait for a shot.

Reference Positions

Backgammon can be like an unexplored landscape where something new and unseen pops up. But it's also full of familiar ground or positions that we see again and again. Therefore, it is very valuable to remember some reference positions for these situations. All references are made at money game format (without the Jacoby rule) as this is the most neutral reference point that is applicable to both money and match play.

From the reference position, you can adjust up and down according to the score. Let's say the reference position outlines a small take and you are playing a match at a score where you need to take less. With this in mind, you will know that you should probably pass. You can also compare your specific position to the reference position. Is your position better or worse than the reference position? Slight changes to a reference position will often reveal the correct cube action in the specific position you see in a match.

5 taken off versus speed board

Very small double for White. Very small pass. Smallest change for white leads to big no double/take. Notice it's better to have the spare checkers on the back points.

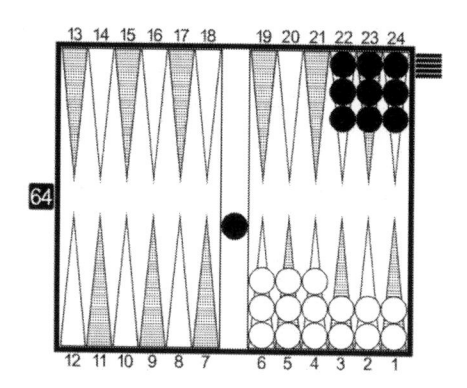

Doubling a back game

Usually, it's very difficult to find the precise point to double and take a back game. Slight changes can affect the correct cube actions. However, you often need to have at most four well-diversified points in front of the anchors to double. Here you see a small double and a tiny pass:

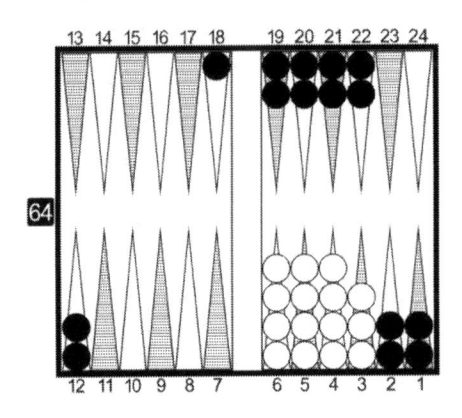

Blockade versus Blockade

A pragmatic rule that you may often hear is that a blockade versus a blockade is usually a Double/Take. We shouldn't settle for such a simple rule. In the three positions below you will see how the pip count is very important to consider. In the first position white is 16 pips behind, the second 12 pips behind and finally 6 pips behind. The first is a Double/Pass, the second a small Double/Small Take, and the last a huge No Double/Take. As you can see it is important to be BEHIND in the race in blockade versus blockade and have enough pips to play in the outfield.

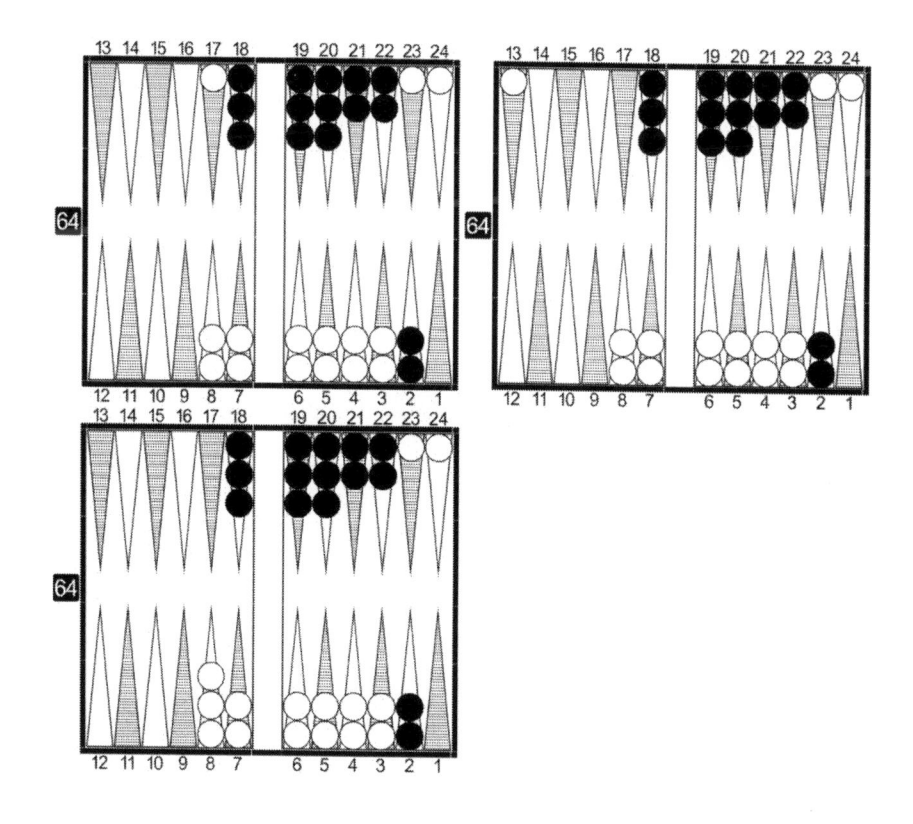

One man back double

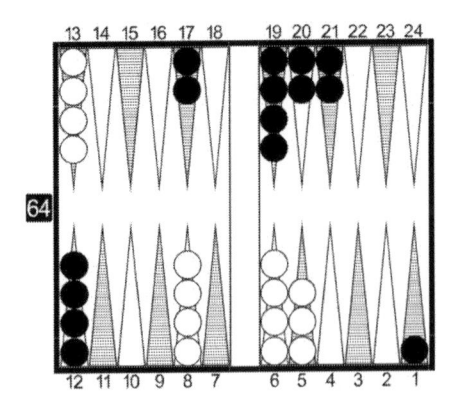

A one-man back position is a bit like a waiting game, but with a policeman checker. What you should realize is that the position is not good enough to double as a pure race as we are not ahead 10%, but we more winning strategies than the race. We can block or start a blitz. Black can still take easily as he can wait for a shot or get lucky in the race. In one man back Black has to take if he is far behind in the race! Small double/big take.

Waiting game - smallest take

Double/very small take, 28 pips ahead for white. The worst possible holding game where you can still take.

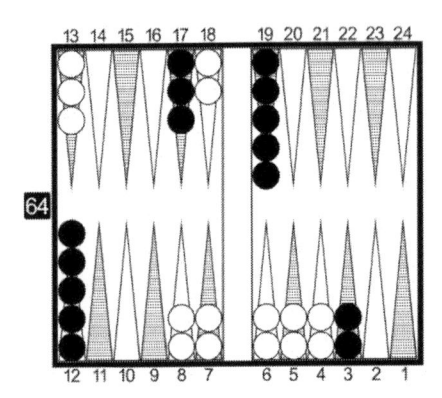

Waiting game - smallest double

Very small double/take. 20 pips ahead for white.

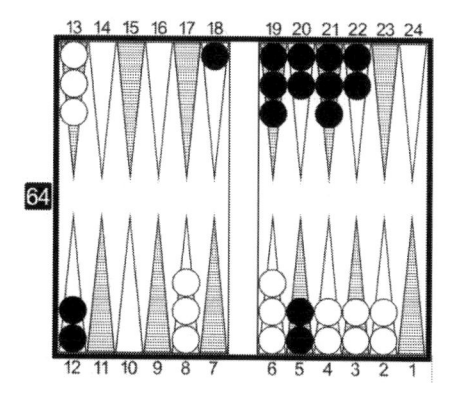

Race

This is a trick! There are no references! You have to count the race every time.

Quizzes

Many of these positions are from real games and are errors made by other players! You might have made the same mistakes. Let's analyze them and map out the proper way to think.

Remember that our framework for analyzing always starts with identifying the proper strategies to choose and from there we use other concepts to figure out the correct move. Let's begin!

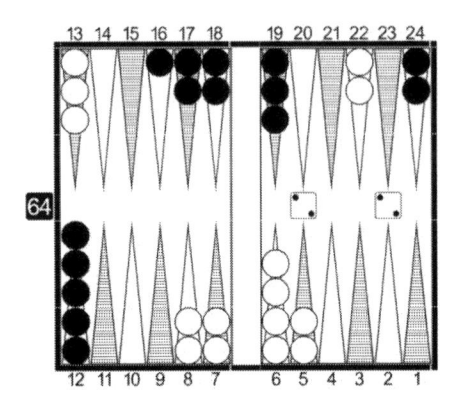

You're down in the race. If you come up with the anchor black is going to have an easy time clearing the 13 and bringing everything in. If you stay back you will get more shots with the gap on the 5 and 4. Play 13/9, 6/4(2).

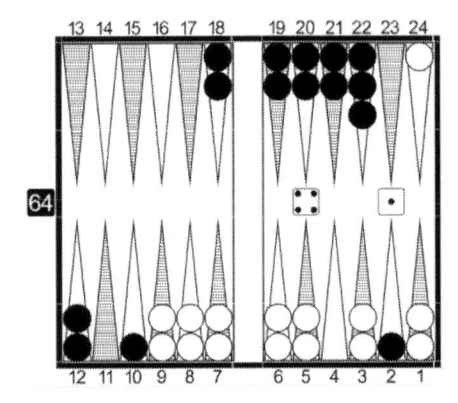

This is difficult if you do not know the basic fact of how difficult it is to escape a blockade. A beginner might be tempted to hit from 7/2, but that would be extremely bad! The way to think about these valuable "step-ups" to the edge of a blockade is to think of them as being more valuable than a good hit. Simply step up to the 23-point and play 9/5 with the four.

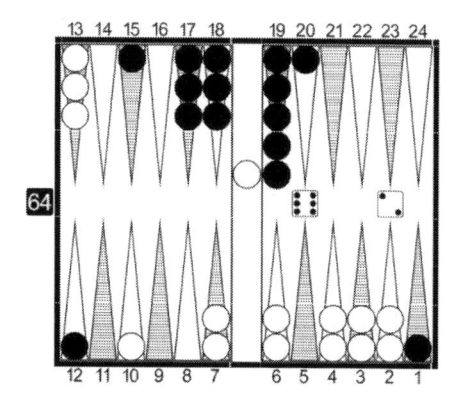

Here the race is 118 for White and 127 for Black. Should we enter and play 13/7 or 7/1*? We have what looks like a lot of nice blocking points so we might be tempted to not hit. But as we know we should often go for at blitz when we are ahead in the race. Furthermore, we have a "strong" position compared to Black and many delicious blots to pick up. If Black hits us back when will probably have many chances to hit back due to our relatively strong board compared to Black. No doubt hit!

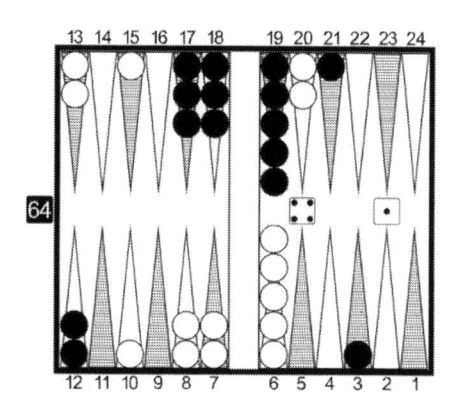

I love this position. Many players would play the safe play 15/10 thereby making a new point and playing a blot to safety. But it's wrong! If we play the much less obvious 13/9, 10/9 we get a great blockade with lots of pure points in a row and block any direct jumping out numbers for Black. You might have not thought it, but this play is actually correct. After our play we are still well behind in the race, we have a high anchor and there is a blot in Blacks home board, so getting hit is not dangerous.

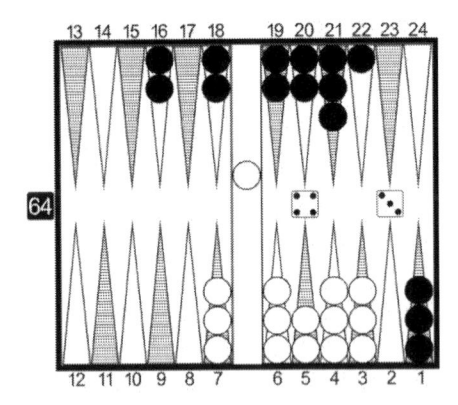

Here White is ahead 46 pips before the hit from the bar. This would imply that we should play on the race or make a blitz. Since Black has an anchor we can't finish a blitz so that's out of the question. Instead, we could play the quiet 7/3 and hope for a 5 in the next roll to jump out. However, this would be wrong. What we have here is a very tactical position - strategy is not that important. Instead, we should play 6/2. If Black hits us back we might dance and not enter, but that's not a problem because Black will almost never escape his 4(!) checkers from our 5 point blockade! If he enters he will most likely have to break his own points and destroy his blockade making it easy for us to escape. bar/22*, 6/2 is correct by far!

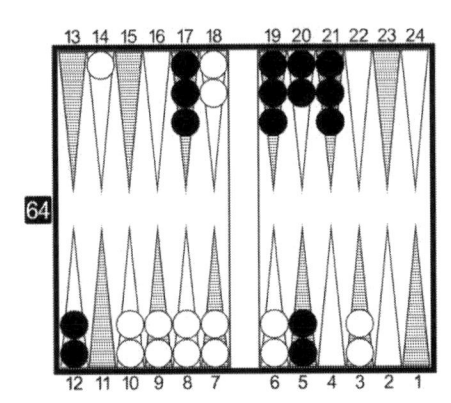

Double or no double? White is behind 6 pips. We have black trapped behind our lovely blockade and we have a nice high anchor. It looks a lot like we have a waiting game plus a blockade. The problem here is that the race is so equal that we lack timing for having a blockade. We will have to break it before it gets to have any power over our opponent. We could call this a "fake blockade" because it looks like we have a blockade, but in reality, it won't have much power unless Black rolls doubles. Black can just play his other checkers and wait until we break some blockade points. Gigantic no double.

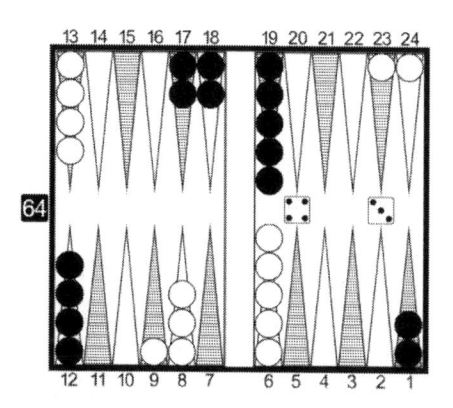

Here we have a nice opening position. Should we make the 20-point or our 5-point? Often it's advised to make the "golden" 5-point without much thinking. However, the 20-point is, all else being equal, only slightly less awesome to have. Here Black has a slightly "stronger" position which actually tends toward making the 20. Furthermore, we would have a strange stripped position if we made the 5-point. In the opening, it's nice to start using the big stacks of checkers on the midpoint and 6-point. It would be more "natural" to making our 5-point using a checker from the stacked 6-point. Normally being ahead in the race makes an anchor a little less important, but we will only be ahead 4 pips after our move. So all in all, we should make the 20-points.

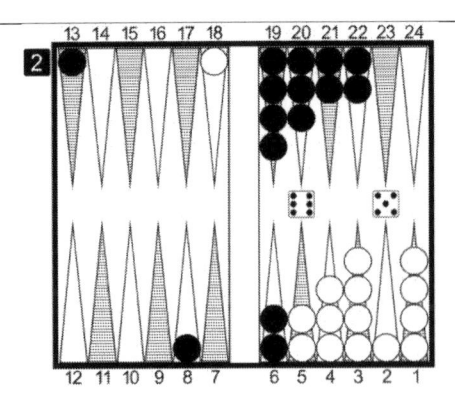

Do you remember the concept of cube efficiency? We talked about how it's important to not win too many points in a match because we risk too much compared to the points we need to win. For example, we shouldn't win 4 points if we only need 1 point to win. Here efficiency is related to the correct checker play. Let's first imagine that we were playing a match and the score is 0-0 to 5. If we get a gammon we will win 4 points - that would be delightful. The correct play is to go for a gammon by hitting and playing to 7. Then Black would have 13 rolls that hit us from the bar - 11 that hit on the 2-point + 61 = 13 (remember that a roll counts twice except the doubles).

Now imagine that we only needed one point to win. Why would we go for a gammon? That's right...we wouldn't! If we don't hit here there would only be 11 hitting numbers for Black as he would hit us from our 6-point and not from the bar. In a non-gammon scenario, we would play 18/7 as it minimizes hitting numbers. After the play, we would be so far ahead in the race that Black has virtually no chance to win it.

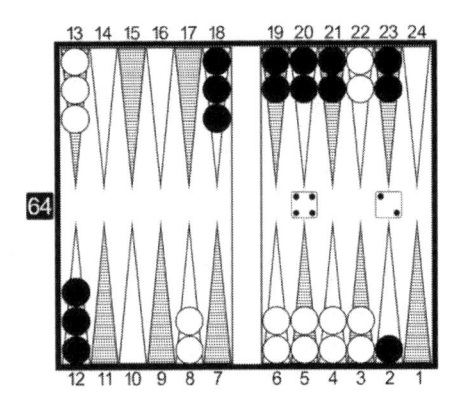

Here we are 18 pips behind. The alternatives are either blitz or block. The race clearly dictates that a blitz is not the way to go. However, it does feel a little risky to play 13/7 to build the last hole in our blockade. If we hit from 8/2* Black can still enter with 20 numbers and if we're hit back we're primed ourselves. If Black enters we are also nowhere close to a winning position. If we slot on the 7-point we are only hit by 11 numbers and when we are missed we will be clear favorites.

The slot on the 7-point is actually best by a huge margin! Hitting is a big blunder!

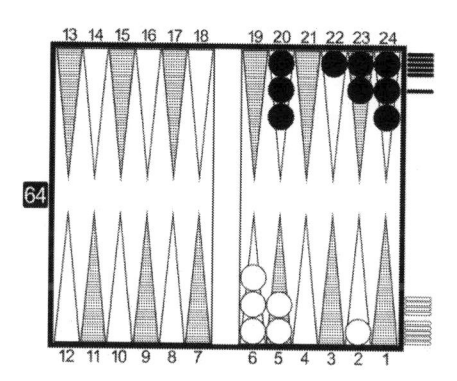

White's pip count is 30, 25 for Black. Keith count alert! We are 5 pips BEHIND in the race. Could this possibly be a double? Let's make a Keith count. We have +1 from the empty space on the 4-point. Our running total is 30+1 and then we divide by 7 and throw away the remainder and add this number to our total (because we're on roll). Our final is then 30+1+4 = 35. Now let's count Blacks Keith count. There's a lot going on: +2 for gaps on 6 and 4, +1 for the extra checker on 23, +4 for the extra checkers on the 24-point. We don't have to divide by seven because Black is not on roll. So Blacks total is 32. The difference is 3 and according to the Keith count rules this is a clear Double/Take. The computer analysis confirms this!

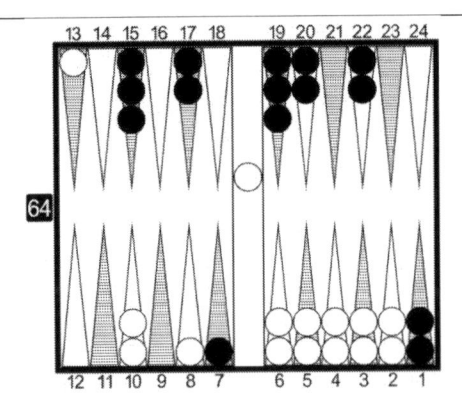

I can just feel sitting across this position just on the verge of rolling and hoping for the best. But hold up! There's actually lots of crazy good jokers we can roll! Remember the O'Hagan law? We need a net of 25% market losers to double. Let's use our dice combinatoric skills to count them. We're assuming that all rolls that enter and hit will become market losers (which is not strictly correct, but almost). First I count the non-doubles and after that the doubles:

- 16, 26, 46, 13, 21, 23, 41, 43. 16 numbers.
- 11, 22. 2 numbers.
- 18 total.

Now I count all the really bad anti-jokers:
- 35, 36, 56.
- 33, 55, 66
- 9 total.

There's a net of 9 jokers (18-9 = 9). This is exactly the minimum number of jokers we need according to O'Hagans Law! And the computer analysis says? Drumroll... Gigantic double / Borderline take! If we don't double here we lose 0.3 equity! That's almost like losing the value of a third of a fish if we were playing for a fish!

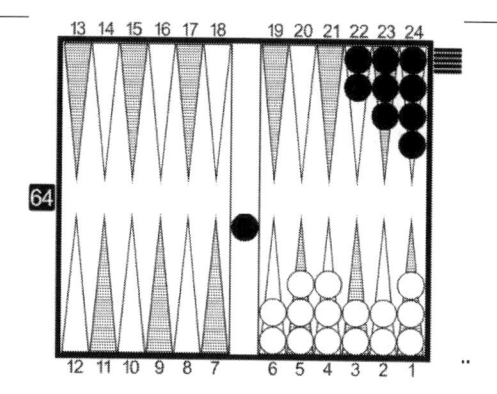

Do you think we should double or roll? We could spend a lot of our mental energy to count the race here. All counts come out saying we are too far behind. But then the blot on the bar also counts for something. But how much? I would be sure unless I knew the reference position I showed you earlier. If you look at it you can easily adjust it to see that this position is very slightly worse since we would prefer to have our three spare checkers further back. Instead of counting I will know in a split second that this is a very small No double / Take. I can just double in the next roll when I have taken off a checker.

More Quizzes

Ready for more quizzes? Go to Facebook and look up Backgammon Galaxy and then find the community tab and join our quiz group called "Backgammon Strategy".

A Special Request

I hope you enjoyed this book. If you did please go and make a review on Amazon! It will let me and others know if the book is valuable or not. I enjoy user feedback ten times more than the few dollars each book earns me so I hope to be hearing from you!

Sincerely,
Tue

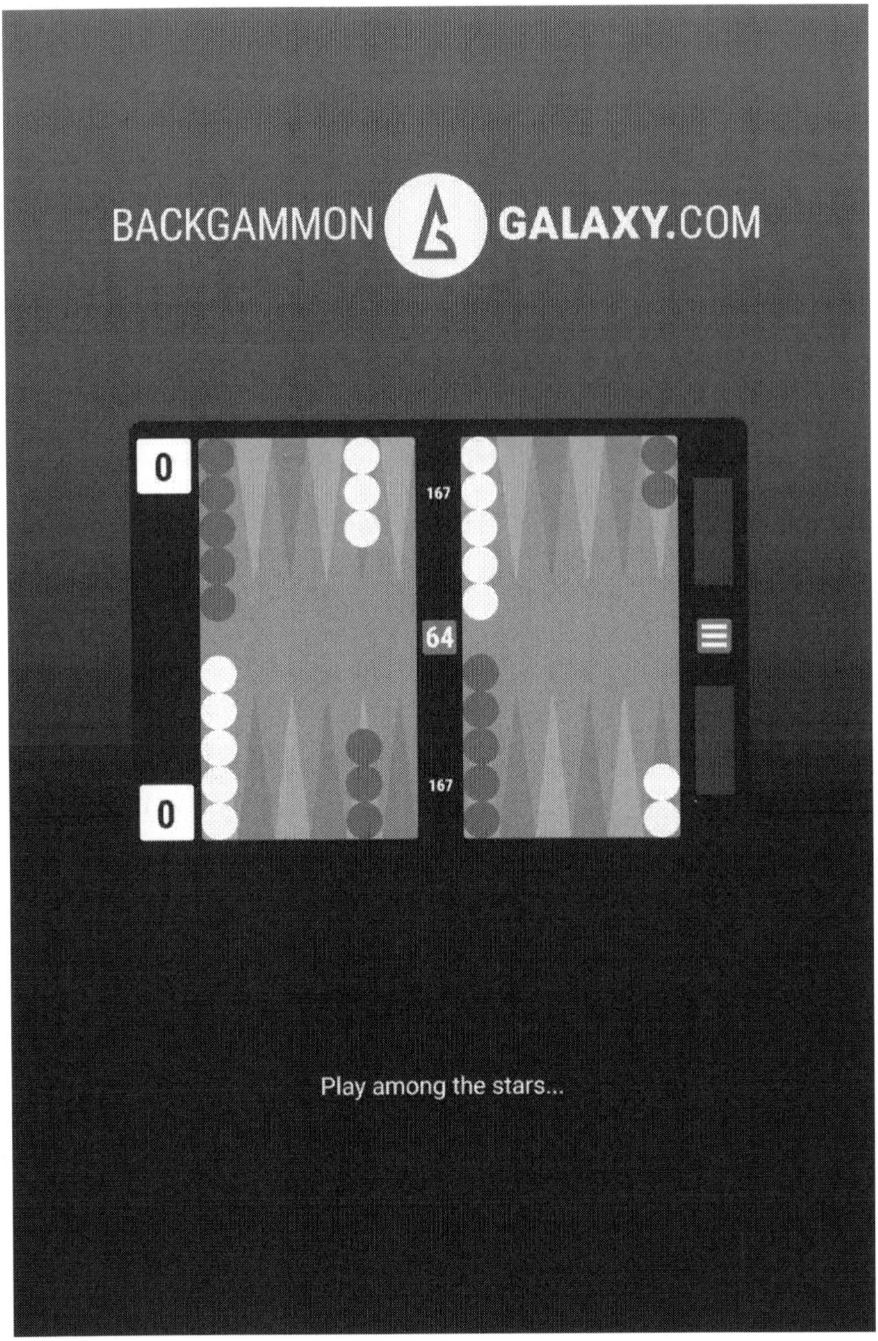
BACKGAMMON GALAXY.COM
0
167
64
167
0
Play among the stars...

TakePoint
A scoreboard for winners!

hello@takepoint.pro | www.takepoint.pro

Printed in Great Britain
by Amazon